Helpers in my Community

Bobbie Kalman

Dalmatian Press

Created by Bobbie Kalman

Published in 2013 by Dalmatian Press, LLC, Franklin, TN 37068-2068.
1-866-418-2572. DalmatianPress.com

CE16257/1012
Printed in China

Author and Editor-in-Chief
Bobbie Kalman

Educational concultants
Reagan Miller
Elaine Hurst
Joan King

Editors
Joan King
Reagan Miller
Kathy Middleton

Photo research
Bobbie Kalman

Photographs
American Red Cross: Talia Frenkel: p. 22
Digital Stock: p. 20 (bottom), 21
Digital Vision: p. 8
iStockphoto: p. 23 (top)
Shutterstock: cover, p. 1, 2, 3, 4, 5, 6, 7, 9, 10, 11, 12,
    13, 14, 15, 16, 17, 18, 19, 20 (top), 23 (bottom)

What is in this book?

What is a community?

A community is a place where many people live and work together. Community helpers are people who make communities cleaner, safer, and better.

Who are the helpers in your community?
Some community helpers are builders,
doctors, teachers, and librarians.
All these people help you.

Buildings and roads

Communities need buildings where people can live and work. Builders construct houses, offices, schools, and stores. They also build roads and bridges.

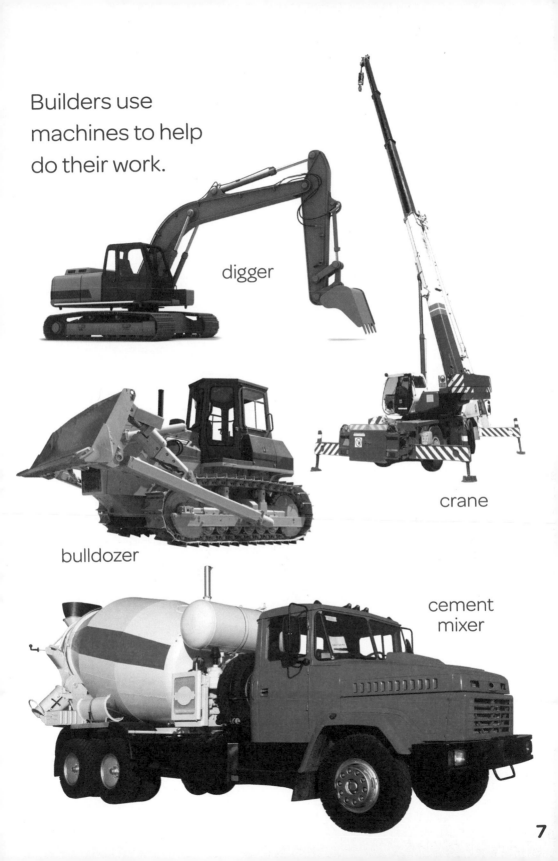

Builders use machines to help do their work.

digger

crane

bulldozer

cement mixer

Electricity and water

People in a community need electricity. Lights, computers, television sets, and many other things cannot work without it. Electricians and power station workers are people who make sure that communities have the electricity they need.

People need clean water in their homes. They drink water and use it to have baths and to wash their clothes. Plumbers are community helpers who put in the pipes that carry the water to our homes.

Teachers and librarians

Teachers make learning fun and exciting. They teach us how to read and write. They teach us math, science, and social studies.

Librarians help us find the books we need. Some librarians work in schools. Some librarians work in community libraries.

Other school helpers

Some children walk to school. Crossing guards make sure the children cross the roads safely. School-bus drivers carry children from home to school and back.

school nurse

principal

School nurses take care of children who are sick at school. Principals make sure that everyone follows the school rules. Caretakers clean schools and fix things. Who are your school helpers?

Medical helpers

Medical helpers are doctors, nurses, and other people who keep us healthy. Some medical helpers work in offices. Others work in hospitals.

Dentists are doctors who care for our teeth.
They check our teeth and fix them. They teach
us how to have healthy mouths.

Emergency helpers

Emergencies are serious or dangerous events that happen suddenly. Emergency workers help find people and take them away from danger.

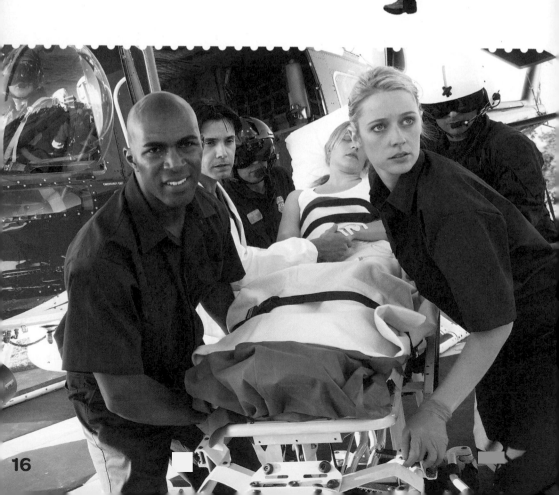

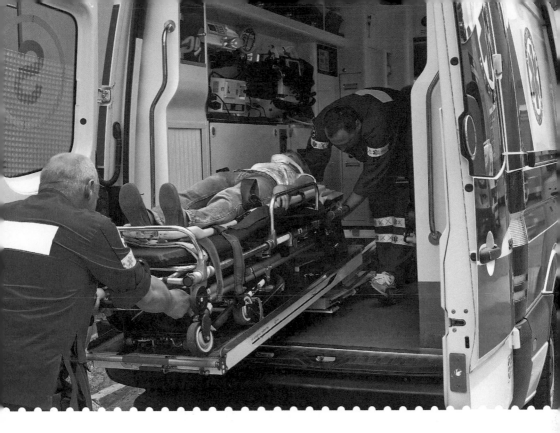

Paramedics bring sick or hurt people
to hospitals. They take them quickly in
ambulances. They care for
the people until
they arrive at
a hospital.

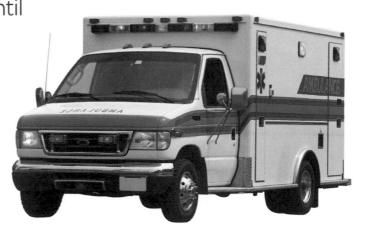

Firefighters

Firefighters put out fires in buildings. They also fight forest fires. They rescue people and animals. They risk their lives to help others. Firefighters drive big trucks to fires.

Police officers

Police officers protect people in their communities. They help people follow the law. They help people who are in trouble.

Police officers talk to children about how to be safe in their communities.

Kind helpers

Volunteers kindly give of their time to help other people. They do not get paid for their work, but their jobs are very important!

You can be a volunteer, too. You can help the Earth by planting trees or picking up trash. How else could you help?

Index